HOW TO LOOK AFTER YO

GUINEA PIG

A PRACTICAL GUIDE TO CARING FOR YOUR PET, IN STEP-BY-STEP PHOTOGRAPHS

DAVID ALDERTON

Introduction

Guinea pigs make great companions and, unlike many pet rodents, they don't have any unpleasant smell. Even if you live in a home without a garden, you can still keep guinea pigs as pets indoors, rather than in an outdoor hutch. You will have to be prepared to give your guinea pig food and water every day, and clean out its quarters every week. You may be able to grow some food for your guinea pig at home, but you will still need to buy some items for your pet's care. Guinea pigs can live for seven years or more, so you need to be sure that you really want them as pets and that you will not get bored with looking after them.

Guinea pigs like to have company and they make great pets – they can live for seven years or more so make sure that you really want a guinea pig before you go out and buy one.

Caring for your guinea pig is fun, but you must remember to clean out its hutch regularly and give it food and water daily.

Making friends

If you leave your guinea pig in its hutch, then it is unlikely to be very tame. It will only become friendly if it is handled regularly. Adult guinea pigs that are not used to being picked up can never be tamed as easily as a baby that has recently left its mother. It is easy to pick up a guinea pig, either by placing both hands under its body, or with one hand underneath and one holding it from above. Luckily, guinea pigs don't bite and, if you're careful, you won't be scratched by your pet's claws.

The more time you spend with your guinea pig, the more it will get used to you and enjoy being handled by you.

Suitable companions

It is preferable to keep more than one guinea pig together, and they are also sometimes kept with small rabbits. Only small types of rabbit such as dwarf lops can be kept safely with guinea pigs. Larger rabbits may injure a guinea pig by lying or even jumping on it. If you have a pet cat or dog you should make sure that you keep them away from your guinea pig as they may cause them harm.

Guinea pigs and rabbits such as this dwarf lop can live happily together. A larger rabbit, however, could harm your guinea pig.

Guinea pigs are social animals, they should be housed together, if possible.

Shows

One of the best ways to see the many different types of guinea pigs that are now available is to visit a local guinea pig show. You may be able to find such events by searching with an adult on the Internet, and by contacting the secretary of your local guinea pig club.

What is a guinea pig?

Guinea pigs are rodents, a group of animals with sharp front teeth that are used for gnawing. Rodents are part of a group of animals called mammals. These animals have hairy bodies, warm blood, and babies that drink their mother's milk. Guinea pigs come from South America. Their closest relatives include chinchillas and degus, both of which are also popular pets. Guinea pigs have been kept for hundreds of years in countries such as Peru. They are kept as a source of food and can be found running around the house. They were first brought to Europe as pets in the 1500s, and have since become very popular.

A guinea pig's teeth grow all the time. Gnawing on a mineral block will help to keep its teeth short.

An unusual name

No one is sure why guinea pigs have such an unusual name. It may be that the "guinea" part comes from the name of a country, either in South America or Africa, which the ships bringing the guinea pigs to Europe visited on their journey. Alternatively, there used to be a gold coin known as the guinea, so part of the reason they became known as guinea pigs may have been that in those days, they were very rare and also very expensive pets.

It is much easier to see why these rodents are called pigs. This is partly because of their shape, and also because of the "oinking" sounds of their calls, which resemble those of pigs. Guinea pigs are also sometimes known as cavies. This is their scientific name.

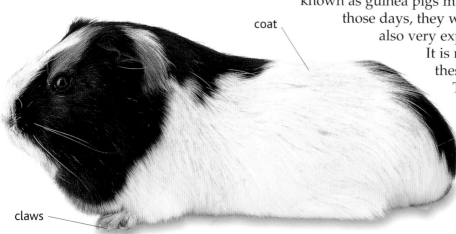

coat

claws

A guinea pig has a stocky body and short legs. Unlike many rodents, guinea pigs don't have tails.

When hand-feeding a guinea pig take care to let go of the food in time, before the animal tries to nip your finger.

Teeth

Like all other rodents, guinea pigs have a very sharp pair of incisor teeth at the front of the mouth, which enables them to nibble their food. Be careful when feeding your guinea pig by hand because as it nibbles down a leaf, it may nip your fingers if you don't let go! These incisor teeth will grow throughout the guinea pig's life.

ears

eyes

nose

teeth

whiskers

A guinea pig can spot danger on all sides because its eyes are positioned on the sides of its head.

Guinea pig varieties

While wild guinea pigs have quite dark fur, which helps them to hide from predators that would otherwise catch and eat them, domestic guinea pigs now exist in a wide range of shades and patterns. There are also many variations in the length and feel of their coats among the different domestic types.

Young guinea pigs stay close to their mother until they are four weeks old.

Males and females

Male guinea pigs are called boars, and females are known as sows. Their babies are born after a period of pregnancy that lasts about 63 days. They look like miniature adults at this stage, being fully covered with fur and with their eyes open. Young guinea pigs can scamper around immediately, and will soon be eating some solid food, but they are not normally taken away from their mother until they are over a month old.

Guinea pig breeds

Today, there are many different types, or breeds, of guinea pig, each of which may occur in a range of colour varieties. New breeds and colours are still being created by breeders, while some of the older varieties are now not as common as they used to be.

A self guinea pig has a coat that is all one colour. This is a short-coated self guinea pig.

Guinea pigs with more than one colour in their coat are called "non-self"; this is a non-self Dutch guinea pig.

Short-haired guinea pigs

Smooth-coated, or short-haired, guinea pigs are very popular partly because, unlike the long-haired breeds, they need very little grooming. Those of the so-called "self" type all have coats of a single colour. The choice of colours is very large, ranging from white and pale shades such as cream and beige through darker tones such as red, lilac and black.

Patterned varieties

As well as the "self" group, there are also short-coated guinea pigs with patterned coats. These include tortoiseshells, which have areas of red and black fur. Another popular kind is the Dutch guinea pig, which has white and coloured patches of fur, and is bred in a wide range of shades.

Agoutis

The varieties that are the closest to wild guinea pigs in appearance are called "agoutis", but even they are more brightly coloured. Their fur has dark and light bands running down each hair. They are different from "roan" guinea pigs, where white and coloured hairs are mixed together through the coat.

Agouti guinea pigs have dark and light bands running down each hair of their fur. They are closest in appearance to wild guinea pigs.

Cat, dog or pig?

There are even guinea pigs, called Himalayans, that have a pattern like that of a Siamese cat. One of the popular newer varieties is the Dalmatian, whose spotted patterning is similar to that of a Dalmatian dog.

Himalayan guinea pigs are marked like Siamese cats. The hair on the ears, nose and feet is darker than on the rest of the body.

Abyssinian guinea pigs are also known as rough-coated. They come in a variety of shades, such as this tortoiseshell and white.

Other types of coat

The Abyssinian breed occurs in similar colours and patterns to other types of guinea pig, but the difference with this breed, however, is that its short fur is arranged in the form of rosettes over its body. Rex guinea pigs have short, wavy coats and are very popular. Their coats feel coarse when you stroke them. Rexes are sometimes known as teddies, because of their cuddly appearance.

Long-haired guinea pigs

It is probably best not to choose one of the long-haired breeds of guinea pig, such as the Peruvian, as a pet because they need so much grooming to prevent their coats becoming matted. The Sheltie is very similar to the Peruvian, but its hair does not trail down over its face.

Sheltie guinea pigs like this one, and also Peruvians, have long hair that needs to be groomed and brushed back daily.

Choosing your guinea pig

Most of the breeds and types make equally good pets, although white guinea pigs are sometimes considered not as hardy as other types. The most important thing is to start out with young guinea pigs, if possible, so that you will be able to tame them.

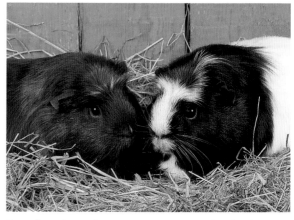

Female guinea pigs, or sows, enjoy each other's company and thrive when they live together.

Any short-haired guinea pig has the potential to make a rewarding, easy-to-handle pet.

Spend time with a guinea pig before deciding to give it a new home.

Living together

Guinea pigs do not like to live alone, and it is a good idea to choose a pair at the same time. They like to huddle together when they sleep and are always close to each other. Trying to introduce a new guinea pig to another already established one can result in the newcomer being bullied, with boars being more aggressive than sows. You need to be sure that the guinea pigs are the same sex, because otherwise you will soon have an unexpected litter.

Where to go

You may find a good choice of guinea pigs in your local pet store, but if you are seeking a particular breed or type, then you will need to find a breeder. Another possibility is a rescue centre, where there are guinea pigs in need of good homes, but be sure to find an animal that is relatively tame. Ask how old it is as well, because once they are fully grown, you cannot tell a guinea pig's age, and you could end up with one nearing the end of its life.

Fit and healthy

When you are choosing your guinea pig, look particularly carefully at the coat, as these rodents can suffer from skin problems, which result in bald patches. Guinea pigs are lively by nature, and healthy ones will scamper around when placed on the ground. If a guinea pig appears hunched up and is reluctant to move, it is likely to be ill.

A healthy guinea pig has a plump, well-fed body and a sleek coat. It should also have a clean nose and ears, and bright eyes.

Place your guinea pig carefully in the carrier for the journey home. Hopefully, you will be buying two together, in which case put them in the same carrier, where they will keep each other company.

Going home

You will need to have a secure carrier so you can take your new pet home safely. Line the base with newspaper, and place a layer of hay on top, where the guinea pig can hide away during the journey. The lid needs to be secure, although guinea pigs are not great climbers. Don't forget there should be ventilation holes along the sides or in the lid.

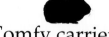

Comfy carrier

You must ensure that your pet is comfortable on the journey back to its new home. The carrier must not only contain some bedding but it must have air holes so that your new pet has air to breathe.

Your guinea pig's home

If you obtain guinea pigs that have been living indoors in the warm, you can move them to an outdoor hutch if you want, but do it when the weather is warm, so that they can get used to colder conditions gradually. Hutches outdoors must be cosy and dry and preferably divided, with a sleeping area out of the cold wind. Site the hutch in a sheltered spot. Inside the home, there is no need to have a hutch. Guinea pigs that are kept indoors normally live in a run with a covered top.

You can keep your guinea pigs indoors in a run with a covered top to stop them escaping. An indoor run does not need a separate sleeping area for your pets, but they should have bedding, food and water.

Your guinea pig's outdoor hutch should have separate areas for feeding and sleeping. The feeding area must have a wire mesh door to let in fresh air.

Your guinea pig needs hay to make its bed and to hide itself away in. It will enjoy nibbling at the hay, too.

Use wood shavings, not sawdust, to line the floor of the guinea pig's hutch.

Preparing the hutch

Line the floor of the hutch or run with a thick layer of wood shavings, which you can buy in plastic bags from pet stores. Add a layer of hay in the sheltered area of an outdoor hutch, or in the corner of an indoor run, to give your guinea pigs a snug bed. Guinea pigs will nibble at this dry grass, too, as part of their food. Do not use sawdust as a cage lining, because this is too fine. It is likely to get into the guinea pig's eyes, making them sore. Buy only good quality hay that is free from dust and spiky thistles.

Get the hutch ready before you introduce your guinea pig to its new home.

An outdoor run

Guinea pigs that live in a hutch outdoors can be allowed out into a run on the lawn when the weather is fine and warm. Special guinea pig runs can be bought from pet stores, but check there are no sharp spikes of mesh which could injure your pet. If there are, they will need to be covered, or cut back. Always place the run on level ground, so there will be no risk of your guinea pig slipping out beneath one of the sides, and no risk of another animal getting in.

Choose an area of lawn that has not been treated with chemicals. You will need to move the run every few days, both to allow the grass to grow again, and also to prevent it dying back under the sides of the run. Be sure to keep the run in a shady area, and attach a water bottle securely to one of the mesh sides so that your pet will be able to drink easily.

You should make sure that the hutch has plenty of hay as guinea pigs love to snuggle in it to keep warm.

Feeding

Guinea pigs feed entirely on plants and seeds. They are very easy pets to look after, especially as there are packeted dry foods available for them, sold by pet stores and many supermarkets. You will also need to provide your pet with a variety of fresh green leaves and vegetables, such as carrots, and sweet apples, all of which should be washed first.

Fill your guinea pig's feeding bowl twice a day with dry food mix.

Vitamin C

This vitamin is very important and must be present in a guinea pig's food. Otherwise, just like us, guinea pigs will develop an illness called scurvy, which causes their skin to crack and start bleeding. Luckily, shortages of vitamin C are rare today, but they can occur, especially if you feed your pet packeted food that has passed its recommended "use by" date. The vitamin C content is then likely to have fallen to a dangerously low level.

Many green plants contain high levels of vitamin C – among the best is fresh broccoli. Guinea pigs will also enjoy a variety of other green leaves, including dandelion leaves and flowers, but avoid plants that could be poisonous, such as any part of a flowering bulb, ferns and some weeds such as ragwort. Also avoid collecting any plants in areas that may have been sprayed with chemicals.

Be sure to give your guinea pig foods that are rich in vitamins, such as broccoli, apples and carrots, every day.

Give your guinea pig some chopped carrot each day to keep it healthy.

Equipment

For your guinea pig's dry food you need a solid earthenware bowl, which it will not be able to tip over. Provide water in a special drinking bottle that is held in place on the wire mesh with a hook. You may also want to give your guinea pig a mineral block, which will help to keep its teeth in trim.

Your guinea pig's drinking bottle should have a drip feed that lets out water when your pet pushes back the ball in the tube with its tongue.

Attach the water bottle to the hutch at a height where your guinea pig can reach it easily.

Your guinea pig's food bowl should be made of heavy earthenware, so that it does not tip over when your pet is eating from it.

Bran mash

A traditional food that guinea pigs like is bran mash. This is easily made by moistening a small amount of bran with water, and placing it in a feeding container. Remove any mash that is left the next morning, before it can turn sour. Breeders also sometimes add a syrup made from rose hips to the bran, to increase the amount of vitamin C in the guinea pig's diet. Or you can add a special guinea pig food supplement to the drinking water, or to mix it into the bran mash.

Your guinea pig will enjoy bran mash when it is offered. Remember to put it in a separate feeding bowl from dry food.

Handling

It is very easy to tame your guinea pig so that it takes food from your hand. Allow your pet to settle down for a day or so in its new home, and then you can start offering food by hand. Dandelion leaves are great, because they are long, but slices of carrot and apple are fine, too. While you are trying to feed your guinea pig, stay as still and quiet as you can and wait. Your guinea pig will hopefully sniff at, then nibble the food.

Offering your guinea pig food from your hand is a good way for you to get to know each other.

Getting to know your pet

At first, your pet may be nervous when you are trying to hand feed it, but if you get into the habit of giving it a carrot every day before offering other food, your guinea pig will soon be eating readily from your hand. You can then try to pick your pet up.

Picking up your pet

Guinea pigs are generally easy to manage and are unlikely to bite when picked up by a regular and confident handler. They are heavy for their size, so be careful not to drop them as this could cause them serious injury.

1 To pick up your guinea pig, place one hand underneath its body.

2 Scoop up your guinea pig from underneath with both your hands.

Catch your guinea pig

Guinea pigs can scurry along fast, and they are not always easy to catch, especially in a large area. Choose a run that allows you to take off the top when you want to catch your guinea pig. Otherwise, you will have to lift up the whole structure, which greatly increases the risk that your guinea pig could escape while you are trying to catch it.

When catching a guinea pig, remember it will head into cover. You may be able to steer it into a cardboard box lined with hay and laid on its side. Alternatively, slow your pet down by placing your hand on its body, and then you can use your other hand to scoop it up.

Once your guinea pig's body is supported it will sit quietly in your arms.

Caught!

Once you have caught your pet, if you decide to use the cardboard box to move it, be sure that the bottom is firm enough to support its weight. You may need to stick adhesive tape outside on the bottom of the box to make it stronger. Also you should never leave a guinea pig alone in a box, because, even if your pet cannot climb out, a cat could easily reach it there.

You may be able to steer your guinea pig into a cardboard box lined with tempting hay.

Cleaning the hutch

Once a week, your guinea pig's hutch will need cleaning out. Make sure your pet is safe while you do this. If the hutch has a sliding door separating the outside area from the sleeping quarters, you can then shut the guinea pig safely in one side while you clean the other, wearing a pair of rubber gloves. Sweep out the old bedding using a dustpan and brush, and tip it into a plastic bag. It can then be added to a compost heap, if you have one in the garden.

Wear a pair of rubber gloves while you scoop out the old hay into a plastic bag.

Safety first

If the hutch does not have a divider of this type, move your guinea pig to a secure carrier, because otherwise, there is always a risk that your pet could tumble out of the hutch when it is being cleaned. Don't rely on an open-topped box: a carrier with a hood is much safer. This will prevent a cat or dog from seizing your pet unexpectedly. During the summer months, you can clean your guinea pig's quarters easily while it is safe in its run.

Sweep out the dirty bedding with a dustpan and brush and put this in the plastic bag, too.

If your guinea pig's hutch doesn't have a divider, move your pet to a secure ventilated carrier before you clean the hutch.

Washing the hutch

When the weather is hot, it is a good idea to wash and disinfect your pet's hutch, having first cleaned it as thoroughly as possible. There are special safe disinfectants for this purpose, which you can buy in pet stores. Read the instructions and then follow them carefully. You will also need a scrubbing brush, as well as a pair of rubber gloves and a bucket, too.

Try not to let the inside of the hutch get too wet, and be sure it is completely dry before placing your guinea pig back in it. If you wash the inside of the hutch early in the morning, it should have dried out by the late afternoon on a hot day. You can even turn the hutch carefully on its back to help it dry more quickly in the sun.

In hot weather, wash and disinfect the hutch using a scrubbing brush and water, and a special safe disinfectant, which you can buy in pet stores.

Water and food containers

Every week the guinea pig's drinking bottle must be washed out with hot, soapy water, cleaned with a bottle brush, rinsed and filled with fresh water. The dry food container will need emptying and washing as well. The pot must be dried thoroughly before being filled again, otherwise the food will become damp and is then likely to go rotten.

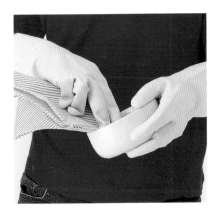

1 Wear rubber gloves while you clean out your pet's dry food container. Make sure the dish is dry, before you fill it with food again.

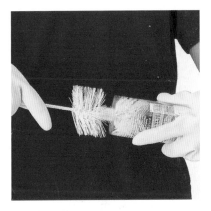

2 Clean your guinea pig's drinking bottle with a bottle brush every week. Use a mild detergent and rinse well before refilling the bottle.

Going on holiday

It is not usually too difficult to find someone to look after your guinea pig while you are away, and some boarding kennels take small pets, too. If you have a friend with guinea pigs, you may even be able to look after each other's pets when you are on holiday, as long as you are not away at the same time!

Getting ready

About a week before you set off on holiday, check that you have enough food and bedding to last your pet while you are away. Some fresh foods such as broccoli will need to be bought just before you go, but apples and carrots can be stored for longer than a few days. Write out a list of what your pet needs every day, rather like a diary, so it will be easy for the person looking after the guinea pig to know what they have to do. This is vital if they are not used to looking after guinea pigs themselves.

If you move your guinea pig in a cardboard box, make sure that it has plenty of ventilation holes and a secure lid.

Don't forget to leave enough dry food and bedding for your pet to last the length of your holiday.

Moving your pet

It may be necessary to move your pet and its hutch to the home of the person who is looking after it. Arrange to do this at least a day before you go, so that should you forget anything, there will be time to sort it out. Finally, leave your vet's details and a phone number where you can be contacted during your holiday, in case of an emergency.

Fit and healthy

As long as you keep your guinea pig's quarters clean, and do not vary its diet suddenly, then it should remain healthy. Do keep a close watch on the length of the animal's claws, however, because these can easily start to become overgrown and will then need to be trimmed back by your vet.

Grooming

Guinea pigs generally need very little grooming, although stroking is actually quite useful in removing loose hairs from the coat. Show guinea pigs, however, need special grooming. Abyssinians, for example, usually have their rosettes brushed gently with a clean, soft toothbrush prior to a show. Long-haired Peruvians, on the other hand, must be trained to stand on a special stand covered in hessian (sackcloth). Their long coats are then very carefully groomed so that they trail down over the sides of the stand.

To make sure your guinea pig stays healthy, look at it carefully every day so that you will notice any signs of something wrong.

Short-haired guinea pigs need little grooming but a long-haired guinea pig should be groomed daily with a soft brush or with a comb to remove any knots.

A guinea pig spends a lot of time grooming itself. Its front teeth act as a comb and its tongue as a flannel.

Skin problems

Guinea pigs often suffer from skin problems. These can sometimes be linked with a diet that does not contain enough vitamin C, but they are more often the result of an infection caused by tiny mites. Look for signs of hair loss or inflamed skin – if you discover this contact your vet quickly as early treatment is important.

This edition is published by Armadillo, an imprint of Anness Publishing Ltd, Blaby Road, Wigston, Leicestershire LE18 4SE; info@anness.com

www.annesspublishing.com

If you like the images in this book and would like to investigate using them for publishing, promotions or advertising, please visit our website www.practicalpictures.com for more information.

A CIP catalogue record for this book is available from the British Library.

Publisher: Joanna Lorenz
Managing Editor: Linda Fraser
Editor: Sarah Uttridge
Designer: Linda Penny
Photographer: Paul Bricknell
Picture credits: Ardea London 7tr /Vanessa Myhan 7br
Production Controller: Pirong Wang

The publishers would also like to thank Rosie Anness, Grace Crissell and Holly Willcocks for appearing in this book.

PUBLISHER'S NOTE
Although the advice and information in this book are believed to be accurate and true at the time of going to press, neither the authors nor the publisher can accept any legal responsibility or liability for any errors or omissions that may have been made nor for any inaccuracies nor for any loss, harm or injury that comes about from following instructions or advice in this book.

Manufacturer: Anness Publishing Ltd, Blaby Road, Wigston, Leicestershire LE18 4SE, England
For Product Tracking go to: www.annesspublishing.com/tracking
Batch: 2913-21995-1127